How to Write a Research Paper

How to Write a Research Paper

by

RALPH BERRY

THE QUEEN'S AWARD
TO INDUSTRY 1966

PERGAMON PRESS

OXFORD · LONDON · EDINBURGH · NEW YORK
TORONTO · SYDNEY · PARIS · BRAUNSCHWEIG

Pergamon Press Ltd., Headington Hill Hall, Oxford
4 & 5 Fitzroy Square, London W.1
Pergamon Press (Scotland) Ltd., 2 & 3 Teviot Place, Edinburgh 1
Pergamon Press Inc., Maxwell House, Fairview Park, Elmsford,
New York 10523
Pergamon of Canada Ltd., 207 Queen's Quay West, Toronto 1
Pergamon Press (Aust.) Pty. Ltd., 19a Boundary Street,
Rushcutters Bay, N.S.W. 2011, Australia
Pergamon Press S.A.R.L., 24 rue des Écoles, Paris 5e
Vieweg & Sohn GmbH, Burgplatz 1, Braunschweig

First edition 1966

Reprinted 1969

Library of Congress Catalog Card No. 66-17791

Printed in Great Britain by C. Tinling & Co. Ltd., Liverpool, London and Prescot.

08 011752 x (flexicover)
08 011753 8 (hard cover)

Contents

Introduction

A WRITER should always be clear about his public, and I specify mine at once. This guide is written for the large numbers of students engaged on one of the fundamental courses of Higher Education today. More precisely, I have in mind the under-graduate or student reading for the Diploma in Technology, Diploma in Art and Design, or a Diploma in Education. Such students have at least one thing in common. At some time in their course, usually in the third year, they have to present a rather long and formal paper. Its terms of reference may vary widely. It may be called a Research Paper, or thesis, or even dissertation. Its objective may be a neutral compilation of fact, or the achieve-ment of original conclusions. Its length may range from two to perhaps five thousand words. But in all cases the writer will be expected to introduce himself to the scholarly disciplines. That is, he will have to draw on a reasonably wide range of recognized authorities; learn something of the techniques of getting the most out of a library; sustain the labour of taking accurate and relevant notes over a long period; digest them into a shapely and lucid whole; and present them with due respect for the acknowledged conventions of documentation.

Now this is hard. It is hard enough for the mature scholars with a weight of research experience behind them. Often enough—and it would be easy, if libellous, to cite examples—they rebel against the intolerable discipline of the scholarly yoke. It is harder still for the post-graduate researcher, who is formally expected to bow to the yoke. And it is hardest of all for the undergraduate, who comes fresh to it.

But submit he must. Among the little noticed (as I believe)

1

aspects of the Americanization of our education system is precisely this task. It is standard practice for an American first-year college student to take a course (lasting half a session) on the preparation of the research paper. The course is a formal requirement, and is backed by a wide selection of excellent manuals on the subject. The British student, by contrast, is expected to pick it up as he goes along. He is most unlikely to receive more than a little token instruction in the techniques of preparing a research paper. I know of no guide on the British market that can give the assistance he needs. Yet the preparation of a research paper (let us say, in practice, a paper that goes distinctly beyond the limits of a normal essay) is increasingly a feature of the student scene, as it has long been in the United States. Work which once would have been regarded as the post-graduate student's province increasingly becomes the concern of the undergraduate. My aim in writing this guide is to fill a gap that exists not only in the educational textbook field, but in the educational system as a whole.

In writing it, I have made certain assumptions that I should make clear now.

(i) First, I am not concerned with purely scientific and technical areas of research. These require a specialized and formal type of report, which is outside the scope of this manual. However, it is usual nowadays for Diploma in Technology students to write a research paper as part of their Humanities or Liberal Studies programme, and I have them very much in mind.

(ii) Next, this guide was conceived as an *Introduction* to the research paper; and I have sometimes been in some doubt as to what should be left to common sense. At the risk of rightly offending many of my readers, I have on occasion included material that might well have been left unwritten. For example, it sounds hideously banal to advise readers to take a carbon copy of their work. I know, and I apologize. But I have known students to whom the advice would have been useful. I do not see why experience *has* to be, as Bismarck termed it, "the name we give to our mistakes". It can be passed on. I have applied one simple test on issues of superfluous advice. I have asked myself: "would it have been useful to me, as an undergraduate?" and if the answer is yes, in it goes.

(iii) Finally, I assume that all papers will be presented in typescript, according to the accepted conventions. I have found that this point needs to be argued, so I shall argue it here. Handwriting belongs to the sphere of personal communication. It has no place in a formal report, an exercise in conventional techniques. Every student should own, or have access to, a typewriter—and use it frequently. Few possess handwriting that will bear looking at. Even with them, it is an irrelevant consideration. As for the incredible argument (which I have known undergraduates to raise) that handwriting "shows character", the short answer is that character should be revealed if at all by the choice of words, not the style of handwriting. The only students who can put up any sort of case are those submitting a dissertation in the third year of a Dip.A.D. course. Their script is, perhaps, a part of their artistic achievement. But even here, the same logic applies. The conventions and techniques which a research report embodies will, later, be of direct value. The sort of person for whom a report will be written—research supervisor, chief executive, editor—has not the smallest interest in handwriting. He is interested only in the content, presented in a frictionless medium. He had better be humoured. So one might as well renounce one's handwriting here. One's personality can burgeon in other fields.

The matter of typing reveals in part the philosophy of the whole. The key words in this philosophy are organization, discipline, and convention. These words may not be wholly welcome to all of my readers, and I should perhaps offer a gloss on them. For most students, the English essay will have been strongly associated in the past with imagination, creativity, self-expression, and a somewhat loose approach to form. These are perfectly proper ideas, which have an excellent educational justification. I merely point out that they are totally irrelevant here. Yet, in my experience, students tend to "carry over" into the realm of the research paper, attitudes and aims that have no place there. Such attitudes have their logical extension into the field of creative writing. But in this guide I am concerned only with the critical assessment of existing authorities. The philosophy, then, can be defended thus. Organization is necessary for the efficient allocation of one's time and effort, and for the presentation of a paper whose internal structure is balanced and sound. Discipline is central to the long labour of sifting authorities, and adding one's own critical comments only when these authorities have been fully assimilated. Conventions are vital in a context where the writer writes not for himself, but for a critical public—a public whose face may change (Professor, departmental head, director) but whose standards remain approximately the same. The student will address his paper to such men; one day, he will join them. And this is the true justification of conventions, that they offer freedom of movement within a larger group. The student need not fear that these same tedious conventions are cramping him. Ultimately they will serve to free his power of expression.

CHAPTER 1

The Choice of Subject: Using the Library

In this and the following chapters, I intend to consider the problems of the research paper in the order in which they would present themselves to the student. The first—and, to my mind, by far the greatest problem—is the choice of subject and more particularly of title. The general *area* of study is hardly a problem. The student selects, or is assigned, a field of study such as the 1914–18 poets, or automation, or the psychology of aesthetics. He has to write, say, 3000 words on a topic in which he is presumably interested. But he is nowhere near fixing a *title* to his paper. A title is an exact indication of the ground covered in the paper. It is clear that "Automation", for example, is quite unacceptable as a title. It is far too broad. The topic will have to be defined and limited after some preliminary reading; preferably in consultation with the student's tutor. Even then, the title might well have to remain provisional. Suppose one originally started with the vague idea of "automation", and after some preliminary reading reduced it by stages to "Automation in Britain", to "The Impact of Automation on British Industry in the 1960's". Even this might, on further reading, prove to be too broad a topic to handle adequately within the limits of the paper. One might well finish up with "The Impact of Automation on Office Industry in Britain in the 1960's". The title, true, is getting longer and clumsier. But it does promise to deliver certain quite specific goods.

Here, then, is perhaps the first lesson of research; it can, in a very general way, be planned, but not blueprinted. One simply does not know what one is going to discover. These discoveries may lead to a complete change of direction. So be it; but at least this possibility should be taken into account in the planning stage. It is, then, desirable to limit one's topic *as soon as possible* to eliminate wasteful and unproductive reading; but one has to keep the title provisional for as long as possible. The sheer pressure of notes and ideas has a way of imposing its own limitations or even indicating its own path. The student's own developing interest in one area of the subject may be a vital factor.

Then again, the formal objective of the paper has to be clarified at once. There is, strictly, a distinction between a *report*, which simply retails facts in neutral fashion, and a *thesis*, which definitely seeks to draw conclusions and assert an evaluation of the material. In practice this distinction tends to be blurred. Unless stated otherwise in the terms of reference, there is no reason why a student should not draw his own conclusions from the material studied. The whole matter of purpose, however, is one to be taken up with the tutor at the beginning of the assignment. Since this purpose will inform and limit the labour of several weeks or months, its importance needs no emphasizing. I recommend a thorough discussion of the purpose with the student's tutor, at the very beginning of the assignment.

The process, then, is one of restriction. A field is narrowed down to a title, which itself states or implies the objective of the research. One further factor has to be considered before the final decision on the title has hardened. That is the availability of information. It is useless to embark on a project before satisfying oneself that an adequate range of sources is at hand. The value of *any* work of research depends almost entirely on the sources used —a thought one might well bear in mind before starting on a fascinating but little-investigated field like (say) "The Machinery of Government in 1970", or "Racial Norms in Intellectual Achievement". Even with more normal topics, one has to ask a few brutally realistic questions. Have the books (or papers) actually been written on the subject? If so, are they available in the College Library? If not, can they be obtained in good time? Will it be necessary to travel to another, better-equipped Library? Can one take a book out there, or is it necessary to take notes on the spot?

Clearly, the whole issue of choosing a subject makes little sense until it is related to the available sources. The chief source-gathering area is normally the College Library. So far, I have treated the issue on a theoretical plane, but in fact it will be resolved entirely by the practical situation. It is high time to consider the practice of the matter.

USING THE LIBRARY

A word first on the layout of the Library. There are four areas worth the student's especial attention. They are the Librarian; the card index; the open shelves, containing books arranged probably on the Dewey Decimal system of classification;[1] and the periodical shelves. The first is overlooked by many authorities, but in my view making the acquaintance of the Librarian (and his staff) is a high priority for any researcher. He knows far more about the facilities of the Library than any researcher, and it is folly to neglect the channels to the sources. A student should make it his business to be on good terms with the Librarian, and to consult him about the problems of the research. I have invariably

One ought to have a rough idea of the general classification, and certainly of the classification number of one's special fields. The system classifies books according to the following scheme:

000–099	General Works	600–699	Applied Sciences
100–199	Philosophy & Psychology	700–799	Fine Arts & Recreation
200–299	Religion	800–899	Literature
300–399	Social Sciences	F	Fiction in English
400–499	Languages	900–999	History, Travel, Collected Biography
500–599	Pure Sciences	B	Individual Biography

found Librarians to be courteous and helpful, indeed most anxious that their Library should be efficiently used. The Librarian is the expert, and the expert should be consulted.

Contact having been made with the Librarian, the student should begin his research at the correct place: the card index. The obvious place to begin at, the open book-shelves, is inadequate and misleading. Certain books may be out on loan; others may be held in stock in a basement. Then again, the physical grouping of books on a shelf may not at all correspond to the complexities of a subject. Even a simple case will demonstrate the point. Suppose one were writing a paper on the Greek civilization of the Classical era. One might start looking at the Ancient History Shelves, and discover certain relevant volumes there. But an important work like Ehrenberg's *The Greek State* might be shelved under Political Science (320); Richter's *Greek Sculptors and Sculpture* under Fine Arts (733); and Kitto's *Greek Tragedy* under Literature (882). How can the researcher be sure that his *coup d'oeil* can take in all the books relevant to his theme, scattered around the Library? No, the only way he can make sense of the situation is by going back to the point where he might as well have started; the card index.

The card index is a register of all the books in the Library. A normally-equipped Library will have two separate sets of cards available to the researcher; those which identify a book by the author's name, and those which list it under a subject heading (such as Italian Renaissance, or Shakespeare). The information is entered on a 5 × 3 in. card. (Fig. 1, *see* p. 9).

From the researcher's point of view, there are three items of primary importance here: the author, title, and call number. To those may be added the date of publication, an important factor in assessing the worth of the book.

The subject card is simply an author card with the title or subject typed above the author's name. If one is beginning an investigation from the start—that is, with little to go on but the subject approach—one has to use a little ingenuity, and not be put off by drawing a few blanks. Thus Socialist Party may yield nothing, but Political Parties will. A large subject like British History has certain subdivisions. It would be listed as

England—History—Before 1600
England—History—After 1600
British Empire and Commonwealth

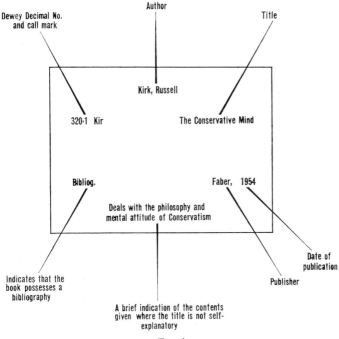

Author

Dewey Decimal No.
and call mark

Title

Kirk, Russell

320·1 Kir

The Conservative Mind

Bibliog.

Faber, 1954

Deals with the philosophy and
mental attitude of Conservatism

Date of
publication

Indicates that the
book possesses a
bibliography

Publisher

A brief indication of the contents
given where the title is not self-
explanatory

FIG. 1

and so on. Finally, it is well to remember that the cross-referencing in the Library may not be perfect, and it is always worth while to try under several subject-headings. Thus, I would investigate Machiavelli under Machiavelli; Italian Literature; Italian Renaissance; Political Theory. One might turn up several cards not duplicated under other subject headings. And the more complex a subject, the more likely one is to need various, and ingenious, assaults upon the card index.

The card index, then, offers the major access to the books in the Library. It would, however, be appallingly remiss to end the investigation there: for two reasons. First, the card index refers only to books stocked in the Library. Second, it does not touch on the periodical section.

The periodical section is, in some ways, the researcher's happy-hunting ground. It is authoritative because it consists of the work of specialist writers in specialist fields. It is often easier to publish a book than an article in the major journals. Then, it offers him information which may be simply unavailable in book form, anywhere. It is principally a matter of the time lag. A book takes a long time to write, and a long time to publish. Once published, it may retain its position of ever-diminishing authority for many years. But a reputable journal may contain fresh and important facts that are months, weeks, perhaps even days old. No book can compare with this authority. One cannot hope to write a paper on, say, "Anglo-Soviet Trade" from books. It would be necessary to consult a journal such as *The Economist*. How is such information to be gleaned? The articles are not listed in the card index. Only the journal or newspaper itself would be listed; and thus one has to investigate the numbers (bound or unbound) on the shelves. The student should browse around the open shelves of current periodicals, which will give him some idea of the astounding wealth of specialist journals. In addition, he can consult two works that list current periodicals classified according to subject. *Ulrich's Periodicals Directory* (an American publication) is "a classified guide to a selected list of current periodicals, foreign and domestic". A similar work that confines itself to British publications is the *Guide to Current British Periodicals*. Once located, the periodicals have still to be analysed. This is not a great labour, however, as virtually all reputable journals publish an annual index. *The Times* newspaper publishes a quarterly index, that is of great value in covering recent events (as is *Keesing's*

Contemporary Archives). The periodical section offers the researcher the prize of being as up-to-date on his subject as it is humanly possible to be.

These three aspects of the Library—books, periodicals, card index—are the primary ones with which the researcher should familiarize himself. There are naturally all sorts of ancillary services (micro-films, abstracts of theses, etc.) which it may be necessary for him to know about. These, in the main, I can leave the researcher to discuss with the Librarian. One point only I would make. In any given field, it is vital to know about the specialist running catalogue (or Index) or annual bibliography, that will bring a comprehensive picture of all the latest publications.[1] The value of this is that relevant books and periodicals not on the Library shelves can be identified. They can then be ordered from another Library, or the researcher may himself pursue them in another and larger Library. In any event, the matter is part of a larger axiom; that the researcher should not believe that the sum of human knowledge, relevant to his investigation, is confined to what is under his nose.

[1] See Appendix on p. 12.

APPENDIX

Each major area of study will have certain publications devoted to listing all important books and articles published on the subject. They are indispensable to a serious researcher. Obviously I can give only some examples. An Art student should know of *Art Index* (published quarterly by H. W. Wilson), which is "a cumulative author and subject index to a selected list of fine arts periodicals, and museum bulletins". In the field of Education, one can cover articles published currently through the *British Educational Index*, published at four-monthly intervals by the Library Association. A student of psychology must turn to *Psychological Abstracts*, published bi-monthly by the American Psychology Association. If the area of study is important, some form of survey is sure to be available. The student unsure of his sources here should consult Robert L. Collison's invaluable *Bibliographies: Subject and National*, 2nd ed., Crosby and Lockwood, 1962. This will list for him all the essential bibliographic information on his own area of study.

CHAPTER 2

Preparing a Bibliography

THE first objective of the researcher is the preparation of as full a bibliography as practicable. The range of this bibliography will to some extent be determined by the requirements of his own research paper. At the outset of this chapter I should remind the reader of the point made in the Introduction that I am writing for a wide range of students. The types of research paper they will be called upon to write will also have a wide range. At one end of the scale a student's first assignment in this field may be a term paper which is in essence no more than an extended essay relying on the two or three books which his library has available on the topic. At the other end may be a much more ambitious venture that can fairly claim to be regarded as a minor contribution to original scholarship. Equally, students in specialized fields will concentrate their attention more particularly on some of the sources I have to consider, e.g. the Art student with visual material. To ensure that the needs of all these students are catered for I have given consideration here to all possible sources of information for even the most ambitious research project. Since I feel that even if one does not pursue the research programme with the utmost rigour, it is essential to know that it exists, I have in this chapter concentrated on the diversity and challenge of the research problem. The student whose assignment is more limited should not take fright at this, but, with the aid of his tutor, select the more readily available sources of information which will serve his need.

To begin with, he must make the distinction between *primary* and *secondary* sources. Primary materials are first-hand accounts, reflections and statements. They are not based on other written works. They are in their original form, without having been arranged or interpreted by anyone else. Official documents, diaries, and letters are the best examples of primary sources; but generally, any sources which can be regarded as the researcher's raw material are primary. Secondary sources—by far the larger group—discuss primary sources. They consist of works which select, edit, and interpret this raw material. Now a thoroughly integrated and well-grounded paper should draw if possible on both types of source. A historian is required to study, let us say, the letters of the Venetian Ambassador in conjunction with a general dissertation on Renaissance diplomacy. Students of art and literature must acquaint themselves with the basic products of the artist and writer before going on to consider the discussions conducted by the appropriate critics. Even students of Dewey's educational theories must occasionally plunge into the thicket of Dewey's prose. All this is obvious enough; but even the most experienced scholars sometimes fall into the pitfall of considering what Professor X said about Z—to the exclusion of what Z himself said. Without making a fetish of primary sources, I do feel that one has to maintain contact with them—however learned and brilliant the discussion by subsequent authorities.

Bearing this distinction in mind, the student must first make out a list of all the available sources that may bear upon his chosen field of study. Later he will select; later he will read, and take notes. But he should not begin until he has made a full, if rapid, survey of the sources open to him.

These are of much greater diversity than is often realized, or exploited. The obvious sources, books and journals, I have already discussed. They are normally the first, and main, source areas. But there are numerous other sources, published and unpublished, that may bear investigation.

PUBLISHED SOURCES

Many institutions issue their own printed material. The United Nations, or the Ministry of Labour, or the Institute of Public Relations, for example, readily advance to enquirers certain pamphlets and brochures giving information on their activities. This material would not normally be listed in a Library catalogue. One would simply have to be alert to the possibilities of its existence, and to explore them. The same would be true of current, non-indexed newspapers; catalogues to an Art exhibition; Press handouts, as of a Ministerial speech during a General Election; pamphlets, news-sheets, and advertisements of all kinds, including handouts from industrial firms. Much of this material is ephemeral; but it exists, and has to be taken into consideration. Again, the printed word does not account for all published sources. Records of the spoken word extend back to Tennyson and Browning; the film is not much younger; the camera came of age during the American Civil War, but for many years previously photographs had recorded the social and natural scene. The various albums, film-reels and phonograph records—whether restricted now to museum collections, or currently available in commercial form— represent a giant supplement to the printed and published sources of the past century.

UNPUBLISHED SOURCES

Writings which have not been made available to the general public are numerous. Diaries, letters, memoranda, rough drafts of writings published later, accounts, church register entries, can be of immense importance. The tendency is naturally for the most important of these records to gravitate towards the major libraries. Others remain to be sought out in Record Offices, both national and local, all over the country; and yet more repose in private hands. Initiative allied to luck can unearth the most astonishing finds even now—and I am not referring to an exceptional field like archaeology. It is not so very long since Dr. Leslie Hotson discovered, in a quite straightforward visit to the Public Record Office, the official record of the inquest on Marlowe's death by violence; or since the Malahide papers were discovered in a loft. A steady stream of less dramatic discoveries continues to reach the public, such as the records of those indefatigable diarists who served under Wellington in the Peninsula. And this is merely the tip of the iceberg. To be sure, the relevance of such material is more obvious in the fields of literature and history than in others. But in *all* areas of human endeavour there is a chance that a letter, an entry in an autograph album, a draft remains behind to supplement or even modify our ideas, based on published sources, of the matter. Whether this material is in public or private hands, it is the business of the researcher to bring it to light if he can.

What is true of the printed word remains true of non-printed products. The various semi-permanent forms that social activity takes—architecture, technology, art—are frequently, of their essence, unique. There is only one Brunel bridge across the Tamar; there is only one Lely painting of Cromwell. But surely such remains can be photographed, and then published in book form? Certainly—but it would be naïf to suppose that such publications constitute any more than a limited and often misleading selection of the material to hand, influenced as they are by fashion, chance, and lack of knowledge. Art History is a good case in point. We know that Dürer was a great artist; we are only now coming to realize the greatness of Witz. The work of one has been much publicized for many years; of the other, not. The writer of one of the volumes in the *Pelican History of Art*[1] has recently confessed that scarcely a week passes without the emergence of some previously unknown painting that has caused him to modify his view. My point is this: there exists a vast corpus of relics that simply have to be seen. It is inadequate to rely on the photographed and published selection of these relics. In such situations the attribute of a good researcher approximates to that of a good reporter—leg-work.

[1] Ellis Waterhouse, *Painting in Britain 1530–1790*, Penguin, 1962, p. xv.

Finally, there remains human conversation. A source does not require the accolade of a permanent form to make it acceptable. There is no reason at all why a researcher should not attempt to approach a living politician, or writer, or artist, to consult him on some aspect of his past work. If successful, the result may be a fascinating series of insights into matters not adequately covered by the existing sources. An oral account is, in its way, every bit as valuable as a written record. If unsuccessful—then one will have tried. And the worst that can happen is that one will be sent away with a flea in one's ear.

RECORDING THE BIBLIOGRAPHY

All these sources, published and unpublished, must be recorded before one can make a reasonable selection and whittle them down to a working bibliography. The conventional method of doing this is to write down each source on a 5 × 3 in. card. For a book, this card should contain details of author, title, publisher, date of publication, and Dewey Decimal or Library Call Number. In addition, the student may well add a light annotation based on a quick impression of the work (which he may have handled physically on the shelves). Thus, on a solid historical textbook published in the 1920's he might annotate: "Looks a readable survey—probably too old-fashioned for a final view—best read first." Of some brilliant but wayward-looking piece of Shakespearian interpretation he might comment: "Check reviews." These quick impressions are immensely useful later.

The point of restricting each card to one source, and one only, is that it makes the later business of discarding and rearrangement a matter of the greatest of ease. The longer the work, the greater the number of sources considered, the more important it becomes to be in a position to arrange the sources alphabetically (by author) for quick consultation. Anyone who thinks this a rather childish simplification should try the task of sorting out a list of a hundred or so titles which have simply been entered, as they come, in an ordinary exercise book. It is not a labour he will wish to repeat.

EVALUATING THE BIBLIOGRAPHY

Now comes the operation of reducing the initial bibliography to a smaller, working bibliography. I shall treat this as an entirely separate phase from the preceding one; but in practice there may be an overlap. It may take, for example, some time to elicit replies to correspondence enquiries. In the interim the student may as well get on with the job of evaluating the sources he has already listed. It is, however, always helpful to think of the research work as a series of orderly, planned phases. Life will certainly contribute its own quota of disorderly, unplannable elements—there is no need to add to them unduly.

I assume, then, that everything within reason has been done to prepare a full list of sources. We now consider this bibliography. It may be quite a small one—on certain topics a working biblio-graphy is, quite simply, all that one can find out. One can hardly visualize a lengthy bibliography for "The Effect on British Journalism of the Three Colour Supplements". In such cases there is no problem. But usually the difficulty is one of restriction.

What makes a source acceptable, or more precisely, preferable? Of the infinite variety of factors that might bear upon this matter, I single out two for special mention: the date of publication, and the standing of the author.

The date can very easily be weighed. It is of course generally true to say that the more modern a book is, the better. One can reasonably assume a second or later edition of a work to be corrected and revised. Again, the writer may be limited; but like all of us he is a beneficiary of progress. Knowledge accumulates. So modernity counts: but this is much more true of some areas than others. Thus a book on nuclear submarines, published in 1958, is of very limited value. One may assume it to contain an accurate review of submarines up till 1958; but so much has occurred since then that the book is bound to be outdated. In this field nothing less than the latest edition of *Jane's Fighting Ships* would suffice. On the other hand, for a thorough and well-documented history of the English Civil Wars, the historian still turns to S. R. Gardiner's *History of the Commonwealth and Protectorate*, the first volume of which was published in 1903. I suggest that one should select from new and old in the matter of dates. One should *always* have a representative of the very latest publications, and indeed aim at a preponderance of fairly recent works. But there is usually a case for including a well-written, old-fashioned work that contains a readable epitome of the orthodox view a generation ago. What in practice one has to do is to cut out a mass of the dead wood that accumulates in libraries over the years.

The standing of the author is a far more complex issue. Often one simply does not know, and cannot know. Reputation is an elusive aura. Just how good *is* Professor X? I can only suggest certain pointers here that the student can look for. In the first place, Professor X *is* a Professor—and this means something, in Britain at least.[1] Then, his work may have gone through several editions. The testimony of his publishers is, to put it mildly, untrustworthy; but if the dust-jacket refers to Professor X's "standard" work, and the book has run through several editions, there is a fair chance that the publishers' claims may not be a league away from the truth. *Somebody* must have bought it. Often enough a dust-jacket (or title page) will make a biographical reference to the background and qualifications of the author, and here again the reader can judge for himself (or, possibly, draw certain inferences from the lack of satisfactory data). Favourable reviews of a previous edition may be cited on the dust-jacket. Additionally, the work may be cited in a published bibliography— for example, at the end of an article on the subject in a good encyclopedia.

[1] It should be pointed out that in the U.S.A. Professor (and Associate Professor, and Assistant Professor) is a title that covers virtually all University lecturers with a doctorate.

All this, however, can indicate only very approximately the value of a work. The nearest approach to the truth must be obtained from the judgement of one's peers. The reviews are crucial, and ought to be studied. It is true that the same difficulties arise with the standards of reviewing, as of writing. Critics can be incompetent, biased, and unfair. But a jury of sorts exists; a consensus exists. Apart from the specialist journals (*English Historical Review*, for example, or *The Times Educational Supplement*), from whom a considered review of a specialist work can be expected, one can look with confidence to certain newspapers and periodicals of established reputation and high standards. Of the daily newspapers, *The Times*, *Guardian*, and *Daily Telegraph*; of the Sundays, the *Observer*, *Sunday Times*, and *Sunday Telegraph*; of the weeklies, *The Listener*, *New Statesman* and *Spectator*; provide a forum for informed contemporary criticism. The list could be extended indefinitely, but the names which I have specified provide a reliable cross-section. True, one can hardly consult them all. But one should get into the habit of checking one or two reviews, especially when a rather extreme thesis seems to be propounded.[1]

And this leads me to my next point in this discussion of the evaluation problem. Most writers have a "thesis"—a point of view which they seek to advance. Put more bluntly, they have an axe to grind. This is well enough; impartiality is an impossible ideal, and one does well to be sceptical of those who profess it. But it *is* necessary to bear in mind the author's predispositions. Is he an old-guard Freudian, or a revisionist, or does he regard psycho-analysis as finished? Is he a Marxist, or merely Left-of-centre? Is he young, or old? Is he (on matters affecting the social activity of a given country) a native, or a foreigner? If it is practicable, one ought to set authorities at each other's throat in one's own work. The great failing in assessing one's sources is to fall

[1] Extremely useful here is *The Book Review Digest*, published monthly by H. W. Wilson & Co.

under the spell of one powerfully-written work. Let the opposition speak, too.

I take as my example a subject that illustrates this clearly. The 1938 Munich Crisis was, and is, an issue of intense controversy. The question is this: was Britain right to buy time, a year's breathing space, at the expense of the Czechoslovak army? The obvious source is Churchill's *War Memoirs*. He argues powerfully and convincingly that Britain was wrong in 1938. But not even from a Churchill should a researcher accept his account un-critically. Churchill violently opposed the Munich settlement at the time; his career was intimately involved with its consequences. He is therefore an immensely formidable, but highly committed, advocate. So one looks to the other side for a statement of the Government case. One would anticipate, and in fact correctly, that the official biographer of Mr. Chamberlain (K. Feiling) would provide such a statement. A more recent defence of Chamberlain has been conducted by Mr. Macleod. There are naturally other historians not passionately committed to either view. The lesson to be gained from this is that no authority is final. None.

Assessing one's authorities must remain one of the most difficult aspects of the research problem. All that one can do in the way of ferreting out information—from one's tutor, or the dust-jacket, or the reviews—is subject to the arbitrament of judgement. And the trouble with judgement, as Housman observed, is that if one has not got it, one never misses it. If Professor X is after all no good, some people will never find him out. But at least safety can be sought in numbers, and in a certain scepticism. Reliance on these allies will save a student from falling too easy a prey to Calvin Hoffmann's view of Shakespeare, or a Marxist's view of Western society.

CHAPTER 3

Taking Notes

THE labour of taking notes requires the utmost exactitude and discipline. Without a strict organization, the process can degenerate very easily into a chaos. Supposing one approaches the matter carelessly—or naturally. One might simply jot down ideas, facts, opinions as they come, into an exercise book, without reference to where they were obtained, or whether they are one's own ideas or those extracted from the writer. One would then be left, several books later, with a mass of unsortable, unverifiable material, some of which cannot even be assigned to its general source. The physical difficulties of re-shaping material which has been entered consecutively into an exercise book are obvious enough; and the labour of re-checking a badly-taken note (what I mean by this term will be apparent later in the chapter) is almost too painful to contemplate. So the job has to be done well, *first time:* and for that two points must be established; the necessity for note-cards, and for a systematized mode of noting down information.

NOTE-CARDS

First, the note-cards. They are the answer to the exercise book problem. The best practice is to use 6 × 4 in. cards. This is because it is convenient to use (of the standard sizes) a different one from the 5 × 3 in. bibliography cards, to avoid confusion, and because there is more room for note-taking on the larger cards. (A very large handwriting might require an 8 × 5 in. size, but normally 6 × 4 in. is ample.) *A single note is taken on each card; a note consisting of one idea.*

What are the benefits of this system? They are twofold. Note-cards can be rejected; and they can be re-arranged. These are immense advantages; for we can say with certainty of all research, that too many notes will be taken, and in the wrong order. The researcher begins by taking notes of everything that he thinks might be useful. Some of the material will prove to be superseded by later material; some will prove to be, quite simply, not as useful or relevant as was first thought likely; some will have to be pruned, or excised, in the interests of space. Waste is inseparable from research. But it is simplicity itself to reject unwanted notes from the sheaf that has been accumulated. Re-arrangement is facilitated even more. There is no way of ensuring that one takes notes in the identical order to that in which they will appear in the finished work. Therefore, one has to shuffle the pack. Very easy: if one has a pack, and not the refractory pages of an exercise book, each page containing several notes of varying usefulness.

I labour the point, but it is worth labouring. And I add that all this applies with astronomically mounting force to longer projects. One might just manage to remain in control of one's material, old-style, if one is writing up a term paper on the basis of a single authoritative book. But for a long-term, ambitious piece of research, covering a variety of sources, the concept is ridiculous. Not to use note cards is evidence of a horse-and-buggy mentality.

The matter of economy is sometimes raised to me by students. It may look superficially wasteful to use a fraction of the space provided by each card. But the cost of these cards[1] is little enough (something like 2s. 6d. per hundred for 6 × 4 in.); and one can always re-use old cards by crossing out one surface, and writing on the back of them. The true justification, however, is that of all economies, time is the most precious.

[1] The cost of a container for the cards is fortunately nil. One ought certainly to obtain a metal or wood card-index cabinet; but a shoe-box will serve very well as a temporary substitute.

THE SYSTEM OF NOTE-TAKING

What should go on to the note-cards? One idea only, certainly, else the advantages of atomization are lost. But the techniques of recording the idea must be rigorously applied. Essentially, each card contains three items of information: a descriptive label, or some identifying phrase; the main body of the note itself; and the reference to the source. A sample card is shown in Fig. 2.

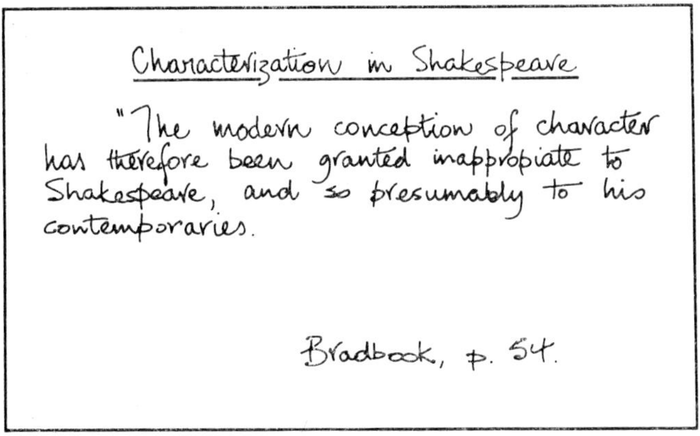

Characterization in Shakespeare

"The modern conception of character has therefore been granted inappropriate to Shakespeare, and so presumably to his contemporaries.

Bradbook, p. 54.

Fig. 2

That is the simplest form which a note-card could take. There is a heading, relating the card to the theme that the writer is pursuing; the note itself, a direct quotation; and the reference to its source. It should be noticed that the source is identified as simply as possible. There is no need to copy out in full: M. C. Bradbrook, *Themes and Conventions of Elizabethan Tragedy*, p. 54. He has already made a full note of all publication details in his bibliography. But if he is using any *other* work by M. C. Bradbrook, he will have to identify the title at least briefly. He might then write Bradbrook, *Themes*, p. 54. The page number is a precise, but necessary, narrowing of the reference. It has to be possible for the researcher to check on his own notes; *and for a future reader to check on the researcher*. The whole foundation of scholarship rests on full and accurate identification of the means whereby one has arrived at one's conclusions. Hence the need to record the details which will later be incorporated into one's footnotes.

Precision is called for in writing out the main body of the note, a matter we have now to consider in greater detail. There are in fact three types of note that one can take: a direct quotation, as in the example; a paraphrase of the original passage; and the writer's own opinions. These must be rigidly distinguished.

Let us now consider the circumstances in which one chooses a direct quotation or a paraphrase. Why does one take the note originally? Because, obviously, one considers the point to be of sufficient importance. But it may be important for different reasons. The original writer may have made a classic, and succinct, statement of his position: it is so well-expressed that the language cannot be improved on. Here a direct quotation is in order. Or the statement, even if badly expressed, may be so fundamental to the writer's position that it should be quoted in its entirety. Again, statements in which every word counts—as in a legal or philosophic context—should be quoted exactly.

There are, however, many more instances in which it is quite unnecessary to retain the exact words of the original writer. Very often a whole chapter can be rendered down to a few succinct sentences. Large quantities of data can be summarized in a few generalizations. One paraphrases a passage for the importance of its *content;* one quotes it directly for the additional importance of its *mode of expression*.

In either case, the form is precise. An original quotation should be followed in all respects. If the text uses American or outmoded spelling, it should be copied scrupulously. An error or fatuity in the text should be copied, and followed with [*sic*] which means "thus in the original". If anything has been omitted from the passage copied, the fact should be indicated with ellipsis marks (...). If words have to be inserted to make sense of a passage, they should be enclosed in square brackets [ ] to distinguish them from the parentheses ( ) that might occur naturally in the text quoted. A paraphrase takes a precise form, in that it is written down without inverted commas. This is not a verbal quibble. The researcher has to feel absolute confidence in his own notes. If the inverted commas are present, that is proof that the quotation is an exact copy of the original; if inverted commas are not present, that is proof that the words are the researcher's own. The positive and negative implications are far-reaching. But, it may be objected, surely the student can tell his own words from someone else's anyway? No, he cannot. Notes taken a few weeks or months previously may have been, to all intents and purposes, written by an entirely different person. It is simply not possible to read one's own writing, after the lapse of some time, and distinguish with complete confidence in all cases between one's own words and another's. Without the apparatus I have outlined above, without the reliance on the exactest techniques, the student will always face a twinge of doubt when he confronts his notes, and comes to write them up in his pages. He is then faced with unpleasing alternatives. Suppose his memory is at fault, he may advance his own paraphrase as a direct quotation—and thus blur or mar a statement where every word counts. Or he may do the reverse, and borrow another man's exact words without acknowledgement, which in the scholarly context is just plain dishonest. Or he may avoid these pitfalls and look up the passage again—which is pure waste of time; he might just as well have got it right in the first place.

So much for the vital distinction between direct quotation and paraphrase. The third type of note, personal comment by the researcher, is an extremely valuable record of stray ideas that flash across the student's mind in the process of note-taking, and which can so easily be lost if not quickly noted down; but it has to be labelled carefully to avoid confusion. The same point applies as before. The intrusion of one's own ideas among those of Professor X may lead, months later, to the confident claim that the Professor's ideas are one's own, or vice versa. Since one tends

C

to assimilate ideas, the delusion is easy. I recommend, therefore, that all personal comment should be preceded by one's own initials. Such a note-card looks amusingly like a fragment of Boswellian dialogue—but the techniques have dispelled any possibility of confusion.

One last point. It is convenient, and often useful, to number one's cards consecutively. This makes possible cross-reference in one's notes: as with an annotation, "See 51 and 73".

A more sophisticated version of a note, then, might look something like as is shown in Fig. 3.

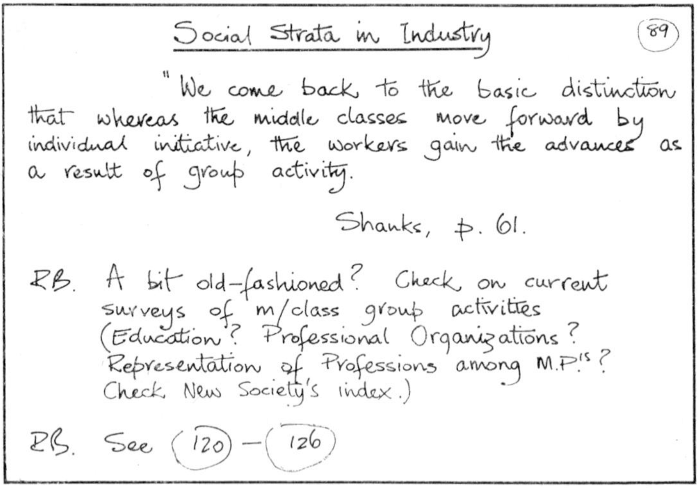

Social Strata in Industry (89)

" We come back to the basic distinction that whereas the middle classes move forward by individual initiative, the workers gain the advances as a result of group activity.

Shanks, p. 61.

RB. A bit old-fashioned? Check on current surveys of m/class group activities (Education? Professional Organizations? Representation of Professions among M.P.'s? Check New Society's index.)

RB. See (120) — (126)

Fig. 3

The note-taker has entered in its original form a well-expressed statement of social differences. At the same time he jots down certain doubts as to the continuing truth of the observation, and adds a few pointers for future reference. Later on he has followed up his own suggestions (cards 120–6) and has been able to add a cross-reference at the foot of the original card, no. 89.

And so the pile of cards accumulates. The more cards in the pile, the more manifestly efficient the whole procedure is; for the sheer bulk of the operation fractures a less orderly structure. The efficiency of the procedure rests on two principles: the atomization of knowledge, and the absolute reliance the researcher can place on his techniques of coding knowledge.

CHAPTER 4

Composing the Paper

THE mass of data has now to be converted to a draft. We can usefully think of this operation as having three phases: making a skeleton outline, preparing an initial rough draft, and improving on the rough draft.

MAKING A SKELETON OUTLINE

This is the most intellectually exacting part of the whole process. Order must be imposed upon chaos, and it is at this precise point that the forces of chaos and order meet. Some two or three hours of uninterrupted thought should be set aside to consider the matter; it is not to be tackled in a stray half-hour; once the material has been set into a form, the mould will be hard to break and harder to alter. The writer should set himself the task of reading, very rapidly and very lightly, over his notes. He cannot, of course, remember much of the detail. His aim is to impregnate his mind with as much as possible of the data. Only then can he begin to shape his material.

Shape implies arrangement and rejection. The latter is hard. It is understandable that a student should want to work in a great deal of his notes. He feels a natural and human desire to demonstrate the full extent of his labours. But, as I have said before, waste is inseparable from research. The student must reconcile himself to this, and be prepared ruthlessly to abandon large tracts of notes should they prove to be superfluous or inacceptable.

Such a decision can only be taken in the light of a constant brooding on the *purpose* of the project. Even now, at this late stage, the exact title may not be fixed. If it is, this title should be allowed to dominate the choice of material; if not, the mental energies of the writer should be directed towards crystallizing the title. At this stage, the problem is normally one of restriction. The writer has a full conspectus of the notes. He must ask himself: "can I carry out the project on the lines which I first intended? Or, with this mass of material, should I not limit my scope?" Perhaps a historical résumé has to be compressed, so as to allow the major period to be properly studied. Perhaps some interesting and worthwhile side-issues have to be abandoned. Perhaps a complex and controversial problem looks to be getting out of control; so the writer decides to play safe and concentrate only on those aspects of the matter that can be adequately handled. All these problems are intimately connected in a chain that extends from title to outline, from outline to selection of material.

I assume these problems to be provisionally settled, and turn to the details of the outline problem. This problem I define as the *search for internal form*. Every topic has a natural (I do not say Platonically ideal) form, and it is the business of the writer to explore and clarify this form. I can best illustrate the point with some examples.

(a) The easiest of forms occurs within historic topics. The secret of history, as Churchill says, is chronology. So one has simply to begin at the beginning (whenever this desirable point is judged to be) and carry on. There may be a secondary problem of judgement in dividing time into phases, but this is no great matter. Thus a general analysis of a historic phenomenon would break the subject down into Origins: Development: Results. The Munich Crisis can very reasonably be judged to start (so far as any historic problem can be so judged) from 1919, the date of the Treaty of Versailles. The period 1919–38 covers the origins of the Crisis, and can reasonably be subdivided into two phases—1919–33 (the accession to power of Hitler) and 1933–8. As for the results, one would certainly have to consider its effect on the beginning of the

War, in 1939, and perhaps take the question as far as 1940–1. After that the question becomes too speculative. So a likely outline for a paper on the 1938 Munich Crisis looks like this:

Part I : Origins (i) 1919–33
               (ii) 1933–8
Part II: The Crisis
Part III: The Aftermath 1938–40

We can add to this a brief Introduction, which states the main purpose and direction of the paper; and a Conclusion, which returns to the purpose-statement in the Introduction and reviews it in the light of the material examined.

All this is pleasant and convenient, and a great incitement to work in the field of history. It is equally true that a chronological approach works well with a variety of topics. Thus a paper on "Poets of the 1914–18 War" might well deal with the host of names by grouping them around Brooke and Owen, representing the spirit (if one likes) of 1914 and 1917. This would be a fair start to the outline problem. Later one could face up to the question: does the quality and significance of the poetry of 1915–16 demand a section devoted to the transition?

(b) But chronology, unfortunately, is not the whole of history. The historian's problem also—and I take it as the model for any-one classifying material—is the ordering of events that occur *simultaneously*. To make his statements even approximately coherent, he must divide the activities of a people into com-partments labelled "political", "social", "art", "economics", etc. He must explain, as best he can, the interactions of these com-partments. This analysis of life is artificial, like all analytical processes; and its justification is that the human mind can only communicate by imposing an artificial order on an incredibly complex mass of data. "History", says Burckhardt, "is the record of what one age finds notable in another." Such is History; but the same act of judgement is necessary to select and order material in other fields.

Thus, the purely chronological outline I have mentioned in my first example is only apparently adequate. It is certainly a promising start. I doubt if a significantly better one can be devised. But it still leaves one with the problem of subdividing within the chronological framework. There the writer must search for an acceptable internal form. In the Munich Crisis paper he might consider the issue from the standpoint of the Great Powers involved—Britain, France, Germany. He would have to consider whether Czechoslovakia, Italy, and Soviet Russia needed separate treatment, or could be dealt with in sections concentrating on the first three countries. Since narrative should not be clogged up by too many pauses for explanation, he might consider some initial paragraphs setting forth (and thus getting out of the way, once and for all) the leaders, policies, and resources of the nations concerned. In all this the peg is chronology; but the determinant is judgement.

Let us consider how these problems were dealt with by Lord Denning, in his famous Report, widely and justly hailed as a model of lucid exposition. His enquiry into the Profumo affair was broken down into four major parts. It will be apparent that the first breakdown of the material was chronological:

Part I.   The circumstances leading to the resignation of the former Secretary of State for War, Mr. J. D. Profumo.
Part II.   The operation of the Security Service.
Part III. Where lies the responsibility?
Part IV.   Rumours affecting the honour and integrity of public life.

Parts I and II together constituted the main body of the inquiry. To have amalgamated the two parts would have led to a confusion of material, and a blurring of the clear narrative line. Part I unfolded the story with reference to the Press, the Police, the Ministers, and the principal persons concerned. It took the story up to Mr. Profumo's resignation. Part II covered the same space of time, but concentrated strictly on the Security Service. It should be noted that in Part I, Chapter I, Lord Denning gave his narra-

tive a clear run by commencing with short biographical sketches
of Dr. Ward, Captain Ivanov, Miss Keeler, Mr. Profumo, and
Lord Astor. Part III, essentially, constituted the Conclusions—
Lord Denning's verdict on the events investigated. In this section
the movement from area to area was logical and satisfying: from
the Press (a public, non-responsible body); to the Police (a public,
and responsible body); to the Security Service (an organization
bearing a far heavier weight of responsibility); to the Ministers,
on whose shoulders the ultimate responsibility rests; to the
Prime Minister. Part IV covered the aftermath; in effect, it was an
epilogue. In all this, most especially in Part III, the writer discerned, and yielded to wherever possible, the natural movement
or flow of his subject. Only in assigning simultaneous events to
Part I and Part II did he deem it necessary to divide the flow of
his subject. The clarity thus obtained vindicates Lord Denning's
judgement. I have dwelt on this example because a study of other
people's analytical processes is most helpful to a student in ac-
quiring the techniques himself.

(c) The terms mentioned in the title usually afford some clue
for the exercise of these techniques. Indeed, some writers will be
well content with simply defining their paper's title. Take, for
example, a title containing the term "Primitive Art". The term
has to be defined before it can be applied; and the writer might
well settle in the end for the title "Some Characteristics of Primitive Art". He might analyse his subject thus:

  (i) Primitive Art exists from earliest times. (*But* it is found
      among savage tribes today.)
 (ii) It is crude, rough, unsophisticated. (*But* some Primitive
      Art is often highly sophisticated.)
(iii) It is intimately connected with religious rites. (*But* how
      is this distinguished from later religious art?)
 (iv) It is functionally connected with religion, having no basis
      in self-expression. (*But* does the controlling purpose of
      Primitive Art negate the idea of self-expression?)

(v) It represents nowadays a sophisticated and deliberate return to older modes of expression. (*But* is not this pseudo-Primitivism?)

Here the writer has laid out his ideas in accordance with a movement of sorts. His analysis moves from the obvious to the less obvious, early to modern. By the nature of his subject he is involved in considering not only the arguments but also the counter-arguments. He has here a rough analytical framework that can serve either as a complete paper in itself, or as a starting-point to a larger project. And he is naturally free to focus at length on any one point—say, (iv)—that seems to him the crux of the matter; reducing the other points to lesser issues that can be disposed of in an Introduction.

Generally, any difficulty inherent in the title should be faced *at once*. And in the above example, the objections to each element in the analysis have been dealt with as they occur.

(d) One final example will serve to underline the need to analyse an issue into parts, and thus pave the way for a later synthesis. Take the topic: "The Flow of Traffic in Large Towns". Clearly, the title indicates a complex of unruly problems. The first step is to impose the simplest ordering of data: that is, "Problems" and "Solutions". The next is to subdivide the problems, followed by the solutions. An outline of the paper might look like this:

I. *Introduction*. General statement of the problem.

II. *Aspects of the problem*.
    (*a*) Simultaneous use of local and through traffic.
    (*b*) Speed limits and traffic lights which slow down the flow.
    (*c*) Intersections.
    (*d*) Parked cars.
    (*e*) Loading and servicing of shopping areas.
    (*f*) Pedestrians, especially at crossings.

III. *Attempted solutions.*

   (i)   The Slough Experiment

  (ii)   Various other solutions tried in Britain and abroad, as:

     (*a*) Urban motorways over, under or round town to take through traffic.

     (*b*) Roads from suburbs with tidal flow (three lanes in, one lane out, in the morning; and the converse in the evening).

     (*c*) Clover under- or over-passes for intersections or, where too expensive, computer-controlled traffic signals.

     (*d*) Multi-storey or underground off-street parking.

  IV. *Conclusion.* General trends and prospects in the planners' fight to keep traffic moving.

The material here is refractory but a logical movement of sorts has again been observed. In the Problems it is from roads and vehicles to people's use of them. In the Solutions the breakdown is first broadly historical to take in the Slough Experiment, and then corresponds as far as possible to the analysis of the problems.

These examples cannot be reduced to a series of precepts. Every topic is a unique problem; it demands to be appraised on its own terms. What the student has to do is to develop his capacity to feel for the natural form inherent in every topic. The student who is really anxious to develop this faculty can find useful case material in the leading articles of the best journals and Sunday newspapers.

WRITING THE ROUGH DRAFT

With the outline before him, the student should assemble his notes in readiness for the rough draft. They should be sorted out into the order corresponding to the outline's demands and the unwanted cards set aside. This decision should definitely precede the actual business of writing. The student should leave himself with the quite clear-cut task of writing up a series of notes, in a pre-determined order, into consecutive prose. It is worth while repeating here that the cards can easily be arranged into this order so that the writing becomes relatively simple.

Little need be said about this writing stage, but one suggestion ought to be considered. The student might well write on half-sheets of paper, each containing a paragraph. The space at the end is useful for incomplete paragraphs, additional material, after-thoughts, clarifying sentences, and so on. Certain long quotations may be referred to briefly, and filled in later. Moreover, the whole paragraph may in the final version be assigned to a different part of the paper. If the student does not adopt this method he should invariably leave some space between each paragraph—and leave a considerable margin. One of the needless frustrations of revising a draft is to find no space available for one's afterthoughts.

IMPROVING THE ROUGH DRAFT

Turning the rough draft into the final draft is a business which needs a cold, critical eye. I recommend that if possible the student should leave his rough draft for a while—Kipling left his for a year at a time—to grow "cold". A few days is better than nothing. It is vital that he should approach the rough draft as though it were someone else's. It might very well be read to a colleague— Swift read his drafts to his servants. The point of this is that it is psychologically very difficult to criticize one's own work. One's blind spots in composition tend to recur; and the tendency to approve one's own work is strong. But if the draft is "cold" it is easier to approach it impartially; and an outside opinion is better still.

In revising the rough draft, one ought to concentrate on two aspects: the verifying of footnotes, quotations, illustrations, and those aspects of the paper in which precision is essential; and the flow, and grammatical accuracy of the writing.

Getting ready one's footnotes, illustrations, etc., and checking their accuracy, needs no explanation. Nonetheless the importance of this labour is central. "Accuracy", said Whitehead, "is the morality of the scientist." It is part of the morality of the researcher.

The quality of "flow" stems naturally from a well-organized outline. But this in itself is not sufficient. The transition from paragraph to paragraph is an important technique. Usually, not invariably, the opening sentence of a paragraph—the "topic sentence"—announces the theme of the paragraph to follow. Often it is possible to make the topic sentence link up with the last sentence in the preceding paragraph. Within the paragraph itself, a succession of guide-words (such as "however", "consequently", "on the other hand", "moreover", "thus", "finally") help conduct the reader across the territory the writer wishes him to traverse. A well-written paper, in my view, is not so much one that is grammatically impeccable, as one in which the chain of evidence and reasoning is easy to follow. No unreasonable demands should be made on the reader. A common fault, for example, is for the researcher to become so immersed in his topic that he refers in his paper to personages, events, and terms that are obscure in the extreme. Unless he can assume a degree of expert knowledge in his reader, this is a provoking irritant. And it is courteous to remind even the enlightened reader. It is also a common fault of inexperienced writers to suppose that because they themselves know what they mean, their reader must automatically do so as well. Hence the value of reading the rough draft to a colleague—and if he knows nothing of the topic, so much the better. The devastating interruption "who's he?" or "what's that?" can remind the writer forcefully of his perennial duty to the reader: to make life as easy and pleasant for him as possible.

CHAPTER 5

The Final Version

FORMAT

In its final form the research paper should be presented as a typescript. Conventionally, the paper used is the standard quarto size (approximately 10 × 8 in.), which must be typed on one side only. The typing of the text should be double-spaced (treble-spacing is acceptable) so that a distinction can be made between that and the single-spacing of long quotations and footnotes. Ample margins should be provided: say, $1\frac{1}{2}$ in. at the left, 1 in. on the right, and $1\frac{1}{4}$ in. at the bottom.

It should be added that literary history abounds in cases of lost manuscripts. It can happen to anyone. The practice of taking a carbon copy virtually eliminates that possibility, and should always be followed. In any event, a carbon has uses outside its insurance value; it enables the task of proof-reading to be shared, and permits a clean copy to be retained, free of marginalia.

THE PRELIMINARY PAGES

The first page is the title page. This simply gives the details of title and author, and if required the name of the course and tutor. Next comes the outline. This is an abstract of the contents, prepared in complete-sentence form. It should be an accurate summary of the major points established, while indicating the structure of the paper. Finally, it may be desirable to add a table of contents. Obviously, certain papers are fairly simple and written in continuous form. No table is here necessary. But if the paper is a more ambitious affair, containing chapters, illustrations, or appendixes, then a table of contents is in order.

ADDITIONAL MATERIAL

The question of additional material (such as photographs, diagrams, graphs, statistical tables) must be briefly raised here. The presentation of such material, especially photographs, is a purely technical matter which must be left to the judgement of the writer. It is outside my brief to offer specific advice in this matter.[1] I do, however, stress that the business of setting up illustrations should be taken very seriously. Illustrative material should be carefully chosen and prepared so that it does give information. If, for example, a diagram relates specifically to a point explained in the text, it is sound policy to submit the text and diagram to a colleague and ask: does the diagram, in fact, enlighten? Does it adequately complement the text? Is it, text aside, self-explanatory on its own visual terms? And this leads us to another consideration. Obviously, the basic virtues of illustration are clarity and relevance. But the student should also consider the possibilities of sheer graphic appeal. Statistical information, for instance, can be represented diagrammatically with great impact. Even a hoary old device such as depicting a single figure to represent a million of the population is commendable. It shows that the writer is making an effort to think graphically; to present information conceived visually, not tied to verbal forms. Such a faculty is not found universally, and many people are, in my opinion, constricted by the heavily verbal emphasis of their formal education. They could well reflect on the opportunities a research paper affords to extend their range of expression. Even a simple graph is a case in point. It is not solely a mathematical concept: it is a visual device. The possibilities of a subject can and should be explored through such visual means. It should also be noted that the technical possibilities

---

[1] Illustrating techniques are well covered in *Technical Writing and Presentation* by Robertson and Siddle (Pergamon Press, in preparation).

of illustrating never were greater. Through the latest techniques of reproduction, colour, and typography, the student can intensify the projection of his theme.

A basic problem should be mentioned. Ought such material to be presented alongside the text, often at the cost of considerable disarray? Or should it be relegated to the end of the paper, and presented in the form of an appendix or series of appendixes? Clearly the latter is more convenient for the writer: the former may be more convenient for the reader. The writer should ask himself the question: does the material throw any direct light upon the point considered in the text? Is it desirable for the reader to view at his ease text and illustrations together? If so, then the writer should make the effort to accommodate his reader. But if the essential function of the illustrative material is to reinforce rather than to enlighten—this applies especially to statistical tables—then he should banish them to an appendix, and refuse to allow them to clutter up his text.

DOCUMENTATION: FOOTNOTES

The major problem in the final presentation of the text is the matter of documentation. The central issue is quite clear. The value of a research paper consists very largely in the sources used. Therefore, these sources must be acknowledged in two ways. The Bibliography listed at the end is a general acknowledgement: the footnotes spaced throughout the paper specifically and individually document facts and opinions referred to. Without this general and individual acknowledgement, the reader would be completely at sea. He would have only an unsubstantiated mass before him.

What information should be documented via a footnote? The matter is quite considerably one of judgement. A fact like the date of the Battle of Waterloo requires no authority to support it. A fact like the casualty returns of the Prussians at Waterloo does. Facts in any way specialized or beyond the run of common know-

D

ledge ought to be documented. So ought opinions. We ought to know the circumstances and the time when an opinion was formed. If it is a scholarly opinion, we must have the full details of the work cited. Clearly a direct quotation should always be footnoted;[1] but so should a paraphrase of that quotation. Finally, the sources of technical information such as tables, diagrams, charts, should always be acknowledged.

Conventions somewhat differ on the form the footnotes take. It is agreed that a single numeral, typed a single roller-space above the line (and invariably at the *end* of the quotation or material to be documented), should draw the reader's attention to the existence of the footnote. This numeral is then repeated at the foot of the page, and followed by a statement of the authority. But the numbering series can take varying forms. It is permissible to number footnotes on a page-by-page basis: that is, given three footnotes on a page, one numbers them 1, 2, and 3, then begins again with 1 on the next page. Or one can number them consecutively to the end of the chapter. Or one can number them consecutively throughout the whole paper, a method sometimes applied to entire books.

Practice varies also on the location of the footnotes. The term "footnotes" is a sufficient indication of the normal placing of the notes. Still, there is a growing tendency for notes to be assembled either at the end of a chapter, or at the end of the entire work. Opinions differ on the usefulness of this tendency. It is certainly inconvenient to have to turn to another page for an authority. Yet a thicket of footnotes at the bottom of a page has little aesthetic appeal to the reader, especially when they afford only a mechanical liturgy of chapter and verse. Furthermore, it is troublesome to type a group of footnotes; one has to allow for the space needed, and it is painfully easy to forget the need for the space altogether. Typing the notes at the end is much easier. In my opinion, the best solution is a compromise one. Some writers divide their notes

---

[1] Except the non-specialist allusion. One does not give chapter and verse for a quotation from *Hamlet*, unless one is writing on *Hamlet*.

into two categories. The first category contains the routine details of documentation—author, work, page number. The second embraces notes that are essentially explanatory—comment, additional quotation, illustrative material that cannot readily be absorbed into the main text. Category two should plainly be at the foot of the page: category one can safely be banished to the end. This seems to me a sensible and civilized discrimination, and I recommend it to my readers. It does, however, assume a distinctive symbolism for each category of note. If the writer adopts this division, he must be prepared to use an asterisk (or some other symbol), as opposed to numerals, to distinguish one category from the other.

The information given in the footnotes varies. The fullest version (which I shall outline under *Bibliography*) is not normally deemed necessary for a footnote. After all, the reader can easily turn to the Bibliography for a full statement concerning an authority. So the footnote usually contains a streamlined version. This shorter version gives the full name of the author (Christian name first), the full title of the work (plus volume number if this is relevant), and the number of the page or pages referred to. Should the work be edited, then the name of the editor comes first. If there is no author's or editor's name available (as sometimes happens with pamphlets, for example) the title comes first. When a contribution to a journal is being cited, or an article in an encyclopedia, the order of the information is author: article: main work. A distinctive convention is employed here. The title of a book (or journal, or play) is underlined; an article *within* a larger work is typed in inverted commas. Finally it is universally understood that the page reference is the only precise and correct way of locating information within a work.

All this refers to the first appearance of a footnote, however. Certain conventional short cuts are employed afterwards. Suppose that the first footnote refers to L. Kaltmann, *History of Alchemy*, p. 76. The next footnote, if it refers to the same work, need not repeat the information. It is correct to write *ibid.* (an abbreviation for *ibidem*, "in the same place") together with the page number. It should be noted that this practice still holds good if the next footnote does not put in an appearance until several pages later. *Ibid.* is always correct, no matter how long the delay, provided that no other footnote has intervened. A different convention is then employed. Suppose our first footnote refers to Kaltmann: our second to another work: our third to Kaltmann again. Now one writes Kaltmann, *op. cit.*, p. 98 (*Opere citato*, "in the work cited"). If, however, one is referring in one's paper to several works by the same author, there is no escape from repeating the title in full on each occasion.

Here are some model footnotes that illustrate in their shorter form the more frequently-encountered kinds of authority:

(First reference to a book)
[1] Mircea Eliade, *Myth and Reality*, p. 69.

(Second reference immediately after the first)
[2] *Ibid.*, p. 93.

(Second reference following a reference to another work)
[3] Eliade, *op. cit.*, p. 107.

(Reference to an edited work)
[4] H. W. Donner (ed.), *Plays and Poems of Thomas Lovell Beddoes*, p. xvii.

(Reference to an article in an Encyclopedia)
[5] "Michelangelo", *Chambers's Encyclopædia*, 1955, p. 371.

(Reference to an article in a journal)
[6] J. Wilczynski, "The Theory of Comparative Costs and Centrally Planned Economics", *The Economic Journal*, Vol. LXXV, March 1965, p. 63.

Certain abbreviations are commonly used in footnotes, in addition to those already mentioned:

cf., "compare".
ff., "and in the following pages" (p. 80 ff.).
l. "line" (l. 25).
ll. "lines" (ll. 13–18).
passim, "in various places in the text". This indicates a number of scattered references to a subject.
sic, "thus". This, used in brackets, indicates that an apparent error is in fact an accurate copy of the source.

DOCUMENTATION : BIBLIOGRAPHY

To the Bibliography belongs the place of honour at the rear of the research paper. It comes last, following the main text, the Appendixes (if any), and the Notes (if they have been assembled at the end, and not typed as footnotes). It is a formal statement of the credentials of the paper, and should be presented in the fullest and most exact manner possible. Moreover, it should be honest. There are lies, damned lies, and bibliographies: it is easy to draw up an imposing list of titles known more by repute than otherwise to the writer. The criterion for inclusion, however, is clear. The Bibliography (in effect, the final Bibliography) should include only those sources which the researcher has used in his paper. It is thus different from the initial Bibliography, which was purely a stage in the preparation of the paper, and listed all possible sources. The final Bibliography lists only those sources which yielded significant material to the researcher. This does not mean that only sources actually quoted in the paper may be cited. One might, for example, read a book as important back-ground material, yet find no opportunity of actually working part of it into one's paper, even though it has significantly increased one's understanding of the topic. Or one might study an obviously relevant source-book, yet draw a blank as far as usable material goes: a great deal of honest research may afford only negative conclusions. In either case it is perfectly proper to cite the works one has consulted. Again, one may use only a chapter, or a part, of a work. The great thing is that the Bibliography should cite only material genuinely relevant to the topic, and genuinely consulted by the researcher.

THE FORM OF THE BIBLIOGRAPHY

All items should be listed alphabetically by author. If no author's (or editor's) name is available, then the item should be listed under the first important word in the title. Several titles by the same author should also be listed alphabetically from the first important letter in the title. This simple classification ought to be enough for a research paper; however, sometimes a mass of detail invites a further classification. One can conveniently distinguish between books and articles. Often a Bibliography is divided into "General" works and material specifically related to the topic. Historians especially like to distinguish between Primary and Secondary sources. And the nature of a topic frequently suggests its own breakdown into areas. For the great majority of under-graduate papers, however, a simple alphabetized list will be sufficient.

Full details of publication are given, in line with the models which follow. These should include place of publication in ad-dition to the name of the publishers. This rule is invariable with regard to books published abroad; but it is permissible to relax it in the case of books published in London. Since the majority of British books are published there, it is conventional for the place of publication to be taken as London unless information is given to the contrary. In the case of the University Presses, Oxford and Cambridge, the place of publication is clearly super-fluous information.

The models follow:

(1. A book by a single author)

Lucas, F. L. *Literature and Psychology*. Cassell, 1951.

(2. A book by two authors)

Collingwood, R. G. and J. N. L. Myres. *Roman Britain and the English Settlements*, 2nd ed. Oxford University Press, 1937.

[*Note*. The name of the second author is not inverted.]

(3. A book by three authors.)

Thorp, Willard, Merle Curti, and Carlos Baker. *American Issues. Volume One: The Social Record*. Chicago: Lippincott, 1955.

[*Note*. It is also correct to refer to Thorp, Willard *et al*. (*et alii*, "and others") where there are three or more authors.]

(4. An edition of an author's works)

Margoliouth, H. M. (ed.). *The Poems and Letters of Andrew Marvell*, 2 vols., 2nd ed. Oxford University Press, 1952.

(5. An anthology or edited collection)

Gardner, Helen (ed.). *The Metaphysical Poets*. Penguin, 1957.

(6. A translation)

Pasternak, Boris. *Doctor Zhivago*, trans. Max Hayward and Manya Harari. Collins, 1958.

(7. An article in a journal)

Ellison, R. C. "An Unpublished Poem by William Morris", *English*, Vol. XV, Autumn 1964, pp. 100–2.

(8. An article in an edited collection)

Vernon, M. D. "Attention and Visual Perception", *Readings in Psychology*, ed. John Cohen. Allen & Unwin, 1964.

(9. An article in an Encyclopedia)

"Numismatics", *Encyclopedia Britannica* (1964), Vol. XV, pp. 615–34.

(10. A newspaper article)

Divine, David. "Will Bomber Command last?", *Sunday Times*, January 31st, 1965, p. 19.

(11. A pamphlet or guide)

A Guide to the Tate Gallery, 3rd ed. Printed by order of the Trustees for the Tate Gallery Publications Department. London, 1963.

CHAPTER 6

Specimen Paper

THIS chapter consists of a short model paper, set out in accordance with the principles that I have outlined elsewhere. The length of this paper is naturally no guide to students, any more than is the number of Notes. Both matters should be determined by the nature and requirements of each paper.

There follows the title page. The essential details include the author and title, together with the name of the tutor and (if appropriate) the course.

THE PILKINGTON REPORT RECONSIDERED

by

John Brown

Tutor......................................

Course ....

Abstract: The Pilkington Report Reconsidered

<u>Purpose.</u> This paper analyses and assesses
the section of the Pilkington
Report on Broadcasting dealing with
television.

I   (a) The Pilkington Committee
          assumed that the power of
          television to influence and
          persuade was immense. They
          accepted that there was wide-
          spread disquiet and dissatis-
          faction over the content and
          effects of TV programmes. The
          complaints they received
          related to the excessive amount
          of violence and low moral
          standards depicted on tele-
          vision, together with a trivi-
          ality of subject and
          treatment.

      (b) On examination of BBC pro-
          grammes, the Committee largely
          exonerated the BBC. They found
          a balanced and responsible
          attitude among the BBC
          authorities, which was re-
          flected in their programmes.

      (c) The complaints cited in (a)
          were, the Committee felt,

largely attributable to
Independent Television. They
found ITA programmes lacking in
balance and quality.

II   (a) J. A. C. Brown represents
            critics of the Pilkington
            Report. He argues
            (i) that the available evidence
                does not bear out the
                Committee's assumption that
                television has great power
                to influence and persuade,
                and
            (ii) that viewers have a right
                 to choose their own
                 programmes.

        (b) Other authorities cited are
            sceptical of the effects of
            television on human behaviour.

III   The position today is that BBC-
        TV has met with considerable
        criticism: while there is evidence
        that the standards of ITV have been
        raised.

Conclusions

The Pilkington Report appears to
have been based on doubtful assumptions,
and it has been heavily criticized. The
situation today is that the gap between the
standards of BBC and ITV appears to be
distinctly narrowed.

The Pilkington Report Reconsidered

The purpose of this paper is to analyse and assess that part of the Pilkington Report on Broadcasting which dealt with television. Part One will outline the findings of the Pilkington Report: Part Two will consider a critical view of the Report put forward by J. A. C. Brown, together with evidence drawn from other quarters. Part Three will review briefly the situation obtaining in television broadcasting today.

Part I

In June, 1962, the Report of the Committee on Broadcasting, 1960,[1] was published. The Chairman of the Committee was Sir Harry Pilkington, and as is customary

the report of his Committee became known as
the "Pilkington Report". Its terms of
reference were, broadly, to survey the whole
field of broadcasting, and to make any
appropriate recommendations for the future.
In this paper I shall confine myself to
the section of the Report which considered
the television services of the British
Broadcasting Corporation and the Independent
Television Authority. Later on I shall cite
authorities who have made general reference
to the "Mass media", which include television together with other media; but the
specific application of all material is to
the content and effects of television
broadcasting.

The general standpoint of the
Committee was revealed in the second

paragraph of its chapter on television.

It opened:

> Nevertheless, many submissions put
> to us about television on behalf
> of viewers primarily expressed
> disquiet and dissatisfaction ... it
> was adverse criticism which
> formed the substance of nearly
> all their submissions.[2]

In other words, television broadcasting was

on trial. It was felt that a *prima facie*

case existed against television, which

would have to be answered.

The Committee went on to elaborate

its view of the disquiet about television:

> ... disquiet derived from an
> assessment, which we fully accept,
> that the power of the medium to
> influence and persuade is immense;
> and from a strong feeling,
> amounting often to a conviction,
> that very often the use of the
> power suggested a lack of aware-
> ness of, or concern about, the
> consequences.[3]

F

They cited a number of bodies who felt that television depicted a world of lowered standards and of excessive violence. On violence, a distinction was made between the "stylized" violence of Westerns and the "realistic" type depicted on thrillers. But the overall effect was thought to be harmful on three counts: that it frightened small children; might incite children to dangerous experiment; and that it encouraged anti-social and callous behaviour. While violence might be defended on purely artistic grounds for a serious play, it seemed too often introduced for sensational effect. As for moral standards generally, many people felt that alcoholic and sexually promiscuous behaviour was given undue prominence in television programmes.[4]

On these counts, together with dissatis-

faction with the triviality and mediocrity

of many TV programmes, the Committee

concluded that there was good cause for

disquiet and dissatisfaction. The heart of

the prosecution view, with which the Report

clearly identified itself, was "the belief

deeply felt, that the way television has

portrayed human behaviour and treated moral

issues has already done something and will

in time do much to worsen the moral climate

of this country".[5]

This was the general position

taken up by the Report, before it dealt

specifically with the TV services of the BBC

and ITA. It soon became apparent, however,

that the general position represented a

condemnation of ITV. For the appraisal of

E*

the BBC's services was extremely favourable.

The Report found the BBC "acutely aware of

the power of the medium".[6]   The BBC was

found to be blameless on the score of

corrupting morals. On the treatment of

violence in programmes, the BBC had laid

down a code of practice as a guide to

producers. Generally, the Committee

concluded "that a sense of responsibility

underlies the programming policies of the

BBC".[7]   The standing of the BBC with the

bodies consulted by the Committee was

excellent. "Representations submitted by

organizations and people speaking as viewers

generally affirmed that the BBC's pro-

gramme was balanced".[8] This view was

supported by a table (see Appendix) showing

the percentage of Peak-Viewing Hours given

to serious programmes (excluding drama) in

the BBC. The percentage was given

as 31 per cent for the second half of

1960.† It was the BBC's policy to devote

about one-third of peak-viewing hours to

serious programmes, or about one-half if

drama were included.[9] The Pilkington

Report made a ringing endorsement of the

favourable views supplied to them: "We are

left in no doubt that the BBC's concept of

balance and quality is sound--both in the

range and treatment of subject matter".[10]

The Report then turned to the

service of Independent Television. The

Authority took the view that television did

not exert a high degree of influence;

---

† The Report does not comment verbally on
  the fact that the table shows a fall from
  the 35 per cent of the first half of 1958.

and the Committee disagreed entirely with

this view:

> We were disturbed by these views.
> For the Authority so greatly to
> discount the effect of the medium
> and hence the nature of their
> responsibilities seemed to us to
> be at variance with general
> opinion. And it runs counter
> to the evidence submitted to us by
> a wide variety of persons and
> representative organizations.
> Moreover, we have already con-
> cluded that, unless and until
> there is a convincing proof to the
> contrary, the working assumption
> must remain that television will
> be a considerable factor in
> influencing values and moral
> standards. The Authority's
> working assumption is that tele-
> vision has little effect. This is
> in our view, a mistake.[11]

The Report dealt critically with

the quality and range of ITV programmes. It

found that they contained too much violence,

and at peak viewing times. It commented

scathingly on the absence of any code of

violence for producers, and concluded that

"the portrayal of violence, in its amount,

treatment, and timing is unsatisfactory

on independent television".[12] Other pro-

grammes such as quizzes were criticized

for their tendency to erode moral standards.

A table was quoted (see Appendix) showing

the percentage of hours given to serious

programmes, excluding drama; this, for the

second half of 1960, worked out as $19\frac{1}{2}$ per

cent overall, and $9\frac{1}{4}$ per cent of the peak

viewing hours. This was much less than the

BBC figure. The Report concluded:

> We conclude that the dissatis-
> faction with television can
> largely be ascribed to the
> independent television service.
> Its concept of balance does not
> satisfy the varied and many-sided
> tastes and interests of the
> public. In the field of enter-
> tainment - and not least in light

> entertainment - there is much that
> lacks quality. It is these facts
> which largely account for the
> widespread opinion that much on
> television is trivial.[13]

The verdict had gone overwhelmingly against

ITA. The major recommendations of the

Pilkington Committee included the giving

of the third channel to the BBC; and the

ITA was to have its powers over the pro-

gramming companies strengthened, with

the objective of putting its house in

order.

Part II

Controversy raged for some time

after the publication of the Pilkington

Report. It was represented on the one hand

as a timely blow against the forces of

commercialization and vulgarity; on the

other, as an anti-democratic, authoritarian

triumph of an entrenched Puritan minority.

I do not intend to trace here the details of

the controversy; but I shall now consider

some of the evidence and assumptions on

which the Report was founded. First, I cite

the criticism of Dr. J. A. C. Brown. He

points out that "the immense power of tele-

vision", referred to on page 2 as the

Committee's fundamental belief, "was based

solely on the unsupported impressions of a

number of oddly assorted organizations,

which not only had no specialist knowledge

of the subject but made no reference

whatever to the vast body of research ...".[14]

He gives some formidable instances of the

failure of the mass media generally to

persuade. For example, the very largely

Republican media of the U.S.A. cannot ensure

a Republican President or Congress; the
Liberal revival in Britain owes very little
to media help; the Eastern European revolts,
political and cultural, take place against
a constant barrage of propaganda. Second,
Dr. Brown points out that the values upheld
as desirable by the Pilkington Committee
may well conflict with the principle of
democracy; for it is a simple fact that for
years, as the audience research figures show,
most viewers have preferred ITV to BBC.[15]†

Violence he sees as a necessary
ingredient of mental life, and quotes with
approval Dr. Winnicott: "If society is in
danger, it is not because of man's aggressiveness, but because of the repression of

---

† R. H. S. Crossmann (Encounter, August
1962) speaks of the audience's "right to
triviality".

personal aggressiveness in individuals".[16]
Social values are acquired primarily through
the influence of one's family, not television. Changes of taste are, he feels, the
result of better education and not television. "Popular taste is always shifting
...", but "television policy ... is the slave
rather than the master of its consumers".[17]
He instances the fact that Westerns have
been dying out in the U.S.A. for years,
without a Pilkington Report to speed their
exit. Fundamentally, Dr. Brown takes the
laisser-faire, allied to conservative, view
of television and of humanity. "The fact is
that the mass media are there to be made
use of, and what use is made of them
depends upon the individual himself".[18]
He has no time for the myth of the workers'

"organic society", or for that of the

gracious standards of the upper classes now

threatened by television. Society, in his

view, is historically and largely vulgar -

and TV programmes reflect, but do not cause

that fact. His summing up of Pilkington is

brutal but hard to refute:

> The judgements of the Pilkington
> Committee, as we have seen, were
> not based upon the Committee's
> own analysis of programmes, but
> upon the "disquiet" and "dis-
> satisfaction" voiced by such
> various bodies as the Association
> of Municipal Corporations, the
> Trades Union Congress, and the
> Ulster Society of Teachers of
> English. What the Committee
> learned from this so-called
> evidence, as Barbara Wootton has
> pointed out, was nothing more
> impressive than the fact that the
> people who are active in these
> organizations do not like what
> they see (or what other people
> have told them is to be seen) on
> independent television.[19]

Other sources that I have consulted do not appear to afford a great deal
of support to the Pilkington Committee's
position. It is true that Dr. Hilde
Himmelweit had told the Committee that "all
the evidence so far provided by detailed
researches suggested that values were
acquired, that a view of life was picked
up, by children watching television".[20]
But the massive survey of the effects of
television on the child, which had been
carried out under Dr. Himmelweit's leader-
ship, and which had been available to the
Committee, had shown little evidence of
these "values" when translated into
behaviour. Programmes did not, for example,
make children more aggressive than was the
case with the control groups.[21] As for

content, the great range of taste made
dogmatization dubious: "... even the most
popular programme or programme type was
mentioned by no more than one-third of the
children".[22] Violence made an impact
depending not on the amount of physical
violence used, but on the extent to which
the child could identify himself with the
situation. And there was a very narrow
dividing line between an exciting and
frightening reaction.[23] Generally, the
survey had concluded, television provided
for the child "security and reassurance ...
constant change, excitement, and
suspense".[24] This did not, however, engender
"passivity" in any of the five senses in
which Dr. Himmelweit interpreted the term.
Indeed, a recent writer, Marshall McLuhan,

has argued that television demands an

"extraordinary degree of audience

participation".[25]

    Joseph Klapper, surveying the

research available on the effects of mass

communication, is loath to make any very

positive statement. He feels that "the

escapist fare is not a prime cause of any

particular way of life, but ... rather

serves the psychological needs and

reinforces the ways of life already charac-

teristic of the audience".[26] His general

verdict, based on a great deal of research

data, is that television can reinforce but

hardly change attitudes and behaviour.

The key issue, of course, is the correlation

of violence on television with actual

crime; and on this no positive statement

seems yet available. As recently as
October, 1963, New Society remarked that
"Evidence of any long term effects of violence in television on behaviour has not
so far been forthcoming".[27]   In short,
there would not seem to be much evidence for
the alleged evil effects of television on
public behaviour,† and for the assumptions
which the Pilkington Committee brought to
their work. An authoritative source, New
Society, indeed dismisses the Committee's
work summarily, by speaking of the "old
trap - into which Pilkington fell - of
producing conclusions without the
scientific evidence to support them".[28]

---

† Dr. Himmelweit reports that television-
  viewing is not even correlated with lack
  of sleep and defective eyesight!

Part III

      The position of television broad-
casting today may be briefly summarized.
It is fair to say that BBC has not, in
recent years, maintained quite the high
position in public esteem which seemed its
assured right immediately after the publication of the Pilkington Report. Channel
Two met a great deal of adverse criticism.
Moreover, the programmes of Channel One
have been under intermittent fire. The
Drama Department has notably failed to win
public favour, and there have been certain
much-criticized programmes (Not So Much
a Programme, More a Way of Life, and Hot
Line may be mentioned). Generally, a
number of responsible critics have voiced
the suspicion that BBC is now competing for

TAM ratings at the cost of approaching too closely the standards associated with ITV. Independent Television, for its part, can fairly claim to have made some improvement. The Television Act of 1963 embodied certain changes in the structure of Independent Television. "The purpose of the new arrangements in the programme field", as the latest ITV handbook tells us, "... was to place the control of networking in the Authority's hands and to give it a more positive role in the affairs of Independent Television".[29] The Act required the Authority to draw up and review a code for violence. Finally, the percentage of hours devoted to serious programmes has grown: The latest figures show 19 per cent for 1956, 26 per cent for 1959, and 36 per cent for 1965. These are highly selective

figures and do not relate to peak viewing

hours. (I am unable to compare them with

the latest BBC figures, because the

classification "serious" is not adopted.

However, I reproduce in the Appendix the

details of the latest BBC programmes.) But

the trend seems genuine enough.

Conclusions

          The Pilkington Report appears to

have been based on insecure foundations.

Both the assumptions and the data on which

the Committee operated have been criticized

by competent authorities, who can point to

a mass of research in their favour. The

present situation looks decidedly different

from that presented in 1962. There is some

evidence to suggest that ITV (whether as a

result of the Report, or no, is not in all

cases provable) has improved its standards.

BBC has lost some public confidence in

recent years.   The gap between BBC and ITV

appears to be closing.

Appendix

I   Table showing the percentage of peak-
    viewing hours given to serious pro-
    grammes (excluding drama) in the BBC
    Television Programme

January – June, 1958	...	35
July – December, 1958	...	33
January – June, 1959	...	$33\frac{1}{2}$
July – December, 1959	...	33
January – June, 1960	...	$33\frac{1}{2}$
July – December, 1960	...	31

(taken from the Pilkington Report, para.128)

II Table showing the percentage of hours
    given to serious programmes (excluding
    drama) in the Independent Television
    Programme

	7-10.30 pm	All	Schools hours
January – June, 1958	9	$17\frac{1}{4}$	$4\frac{1}{2}$
July – December, 1958	$12\frac{3}{4}$	$16\frac{3}{4}$	$3\frac{1}{2}$
January – June, 1959	$11\frac{1}{2}$	$17\frac{3}{4}$	5
July – December, 1959	$15\frac{1}{2}$	$18\frac{1}{2}$	4
January – June, 1960	$9\frac{1}{2}$	$16\frac{1}{2}$	$5\frac{1}{2}$
July – December, 1960	$9\frac{1}{4}$	$19\frac{1}{2}$	3

(taken from the Pilkington Report, para.189)

Appendix (cont.)

III   Table showing an analysis of Network
      Hours on BBC-TV for the 52 weeks ended
      March 27th, 1964

Classification	Percentage
Outside Broadcasts ...	16.8
Talks, documentaries, Information ...	15.0
British and foreign feature films and series	13.3
Drama ...	10.8
Schools Broadcasts ...	8.9
Children's Programmes...	8.2
Light Entertainment ...	7.3
News, weather ...	6.1
Presentation material...	4.9
Religious Programmes ...	4.0
Adult Education Programmes ...	2.0
Music ...	1.5
Sports news and reports	1.2

	100.0

(taken from Appendix C of the BBC's Annual
Report and Accounts for the year 1963-64)

Notes

[1] Report of the Committee on Broadcasting, 1960. H.M.S.O., 1962. (Referred to subsequently as the Pilkington Report.)

[2] Ibid., para. 78.

[3] Ibid., para. 81.

[4] Ibid., paras. 84-9.

[5] Ibid., para. 90.

[6] Ibid., para. 114.

[7] Ibid., para. 124.

[8] Ibid., para. 126.

[9] Ibid., paras. 128-9.

[10] Ibid., para. 132.

[11] Ibid., para. 160.

[12] Ibid., paras. 177-86,

[13] Ibid., para. 174.

[14] J. A. C. Brown, Techniques of Persuasion, p. 148.

[15] Ibid., p. 149.

[16] Ibid., p. 154.

[17] Ibid., p. 160.

[18] Ibid., p. 161.

[19] Ibid., p. 316.

[20] Pilkington, para. 81.

[21] Hilde T. Himmelweit, A. N. Oppenheim, and Pamela Vance, Television and the Child, p. 20.

[22] Ibid., p. 14.

[23] Ibid., p. 20.

[24] Ibid., p. 15.

[25] Marshall McLuhan, Understanding Media, p. 309.

[26] Joseph T. Klapper, The Effects of Mass Communication, p. 205.

[27] "Progress and Problems", New Society, October 3rd, 1963, p. 22.

[28] "Observations", New Society, July 18th, 1963, p. 4.

[29] ITV 1965: A Guide to Independent Televison, p. 17.

Bibliography

British Broadcasting Corporation. <u>Annual</u>
<u>Report and Accounts for the Year 1963-64.</u>
H.M.S.O., 1964.

Brown, J. A. C. <u>Techniques of Persuasion.</u>
Penguin, 1963.

Crossmann, R. H. S. "Thoughts of a Captive
Viewer", <u>Encounter,</u> August, 1962, pp. 46-52.

Himmelweit, Hilde T., A. N. Oppenheim, and
Pamela Vance. <u>Television and the Child.</u>
Oxford University Press, 1958.

<u>ITV 1965: A Guide to Independent Television.</u>
ITA, 1965.

Klapper, Joseph T. <u>The Effects of Mass</u>
<u>Communication.</u> Illinois: The Free Press of
Glencoe, 1960.

Lazarsfeld, Paul F. and Robert K. Merton.
"Mass Communication, Popular Taste, and
Organized Social Action", in <u>Mass Com-</u>
<u>munications,</u> ed. Wilbur Schramm, 2nd ed.
Urbana: University of Illinois, 1960,
pp. 492-512.

McLuhan, Marshall. <u>Understanding Media.</u>
Routledge & Kegan Paul, 1964.

"Observations", New Society, July 18th,
1963, p. 4.

"Progress and Problems", New Society,
October 3rd, 1963, p. 22.

Report of the Committee on Broadcasting,
1960. H.M.S.O., 1962.

CHAPTER 7

Some Errors to Avoid

IN this final chapter I do not propose to break new ground. The points raised have for the most part been dealt with, at least implicitly, in the preceding chapters. Nevertheless, it is I feel valuable to recapitulate the main varieties of error in student papers. My approach is not theoretic, but purely practical. I do not attempt to survey the major possible danger areas. This chapter is, quite simply, the record of what I have found to be the most frequently-committed blunders.

I group my remarks under four heads: Purpose and Conclusion; Documentation; Shape and Flow; Presentation.

PURPOSE AND CONCLUSION

(a) A research paper should be circular in argument. That is, the formal aim of the paper should be stated in the opening paragraph; the conclusion should return to the opening, and examine the original purpose in the light of the data assembled. It is a prime error to present conclusions that are not directly related to the evidence previously presented. For example, a student paper entitled "The Significance of Freud" reached, after an examination of Freud's thinking, the following conclusion: "Because of the application and acceptance of his theories, Sigmund Freud has had a greater influence on both scientific and popular thought and belief than any other psychologist or physician of the past century." Now this statement may be perfectly true, but as a conclusion it will not stand up. The *title*

85

implies at least a look at Freud's disciples, revisers, and opponents. This, in the paper cited, was not performed. The *conclusion* fits the title well enough—but not the body of the paper. The writer was not in a position, on the evidence which he marshalled, to arrive at the conclusion which he did. The student had clearly reverted to his title in making his conclusion, without reference to what his paper had actually said.

Now we have to be pragmatic about this. In a strict laboratory sense, it is necessary to lay down *at the start* of the research the aims and methods. The data and conclusions then follow. But in a less rigorously scientific context, one often starts the research with no more than a sense of direction, and pursues it until a pattern emerges. This pattern will then determine the purpose, which is stated in the opening, and this in turn is pursued to the conclusion. The great failure is not to review the work at the end, and not to ensure that the sequence of purpose: data: conclusions: forms a consistent and co-ordinated whole.

(b) A further aspect of Purpose should be mentioned. A writer should have a clear idea of the audience to whom his paper is addressed. Is it lay, or specialist? The question is important because on the answer will turn the inclusion of much subsidiary material. It is easy both to over-emphasize and under-emphasize the amount of specialized, technical knowledge (and jargon) to be included in a paper. If the subject demands the inclusion of technical terms, a small glossary may be added to the paper. If the subject is of the humanities, but demanding a constant reference to obscure facts, the writer has to consider well how much he can expect of his reader/public. The student's tutor may have no specialized knowledge of the topic. And even a Professor of History, say, might like to be reminded of the Cabinet post held by W. H. Smith in Disraeli's administration. On the other hand, an expert finds it extraordinarily irritating to be bombarded with minor information that he is perfectly well aware of. The whole question needs to be thought out very carefully. The crime is not to ponder the question: "For whom am I writing?"

DOCUMENTATION

(a) This area I unhesitatingly nominate as the chief con-
centration of student failings in the writing of research papers.
I need not labour the commoner failings: lack of dates, lack of
author's initials, lack of the full details required for documentation.
These failings may be ascribed to sloth; as may the simple reluc-
tance to footnote at all. I do not inveigh against sloth: I merely
point out that work produced with such sublime disregard for
the principle of documentation cannot be dignified with the title
of "Research Paper". But these crimes are gross, open, palpable.
They are worse than crimes: blunders. To claim a large Bibliography (without having made use of it), however, cannot be readily
detected, and thus must be termed a sin. I can only commend the
researcher to set down, in his Bibliography, no more than he may
rightfully claim. He may be questioned on his sources by his
tutor, but essentially the matter remains a private one—between
himself, and the Muse of Scholarship.

(b) As sinful, but more readily detected, is the tendency to
pass off a direct quotation as one's own sentence—presumably, to
avoid the tedium of appending a footnote. Since sloth is by no
means to be correlated with intelligence, it is interesting to
observe that writers guilty of this fault quite often carry it out
inefficiently. A sudden change of style can be quite easily detected
by a perceptive reader. It is not difficult to guess the truth in the
following extract: "What's wrong with advertising? I do not see
that the critics have such a good case. It is not clear how far the
widespread anxiety and hostility among the intellectuals, literary
and cultural critics of advertising is shared by the general public.
Further, it is not clear how far the fears that advertising inculcates
wrong values and habits are supported by evidence." No great
literary gifts are needed to perceive that the first two, and last
two sentences in this extract are written by different people.
The colloquial, decidedly non-literary phrasing of the first part
contrasts painfully with the careful, mandarin-type prose of the

second. That is why I regard such a practice as unintelligent. Not all styles contrast so obviously; but tutors easily acquire the knack of spotting a word, a phrase, a sentence that is not in key with the rest of the paper. And the effort required to dovetail styles could more simply be directed to inserting quotation marks, and setting down a footnote.

(c) Even sound and conscientious students, who would not dream of concealing a direct quotation, are sometimes blind to the demands of footnoting. It is *not* sufficient to paraphrase all sources, and write up the paper, in one's own words, devoid of footnotes. The Bibliography lists all the sources used, but cannot relate them to the specific points made in the paper. Where controversial matters are concerned, it is more than ever important to know *which* authorities are making the point. A paper on the Schlieffen Plan, for example, can make a point far more tellingly if it relates this point to Herr Ritter (the latest, German, historian) and does not leave the point to be vaguely associated with an English historian of the 1920's. The whole value of the paper depends on the precise identification of each source used in the argument. One can say, then, that it is a quite basic failing to neglect this identification at all key points.

(d) A final weakness in this department is the inadequacy of the authorities cited. Perhaps three important types of inadequacy may be discerned.

(i) First, the sources may be out of date. One may say dogmatically that all Bibliographies should contain several sources published for the first time in the 1960's. And however classic its stature, there are few works published before (say) 1950 that do not stand in some need of revision. Such works may be leaned on heavily, but not trusted absolutely. They should be checked against later works, articles, and critical reviews. However decisive the influence of a seminal work such as Burckhardt's *The Civilization of the Renaissance in Italy* (1860) may be, it is folly to regard it as the epitome of modern thinking on the Renaissance. Even a much more recent seminal work like Whyte's *The Organization Man* (1955) stands in some need of being reconsidered. The student should be aware that scholars, not least sociologists, have invested heavily in change.

(ii) Second, there is the inadequacy of one-sidedness. This is fatally easy to yield to. Some writers become influential because they write well; others because they write badly. It is easy to fall under the spell of Macaulay's view of events, because he writes so well. It is equally easy to accept the ideas of Hegel or Dewey, because they are virtually impossible to read. However they are cast, the researcher should coldly resist all spells. He ought to aim at a spread of authorities. Especially he ought to remember that certain subjects are under quite fundamental attacks. He cannot, for example, regard psycho-analysis as a territory owned communally in perpetuity, and disputed over, by Freudians, Adlerians, Stekelites, and so on. He should bear in mind that it is perfectly possible to dismiss psycho-analysis as an aberration in the history of psychology. (Cf. the attacks, for example, of Professor Eysenck, in *The Uses and Abuses of Psychology*, and of Alasdair McIntyre in *Encounter*, May 1965.) The root failure here is perhaps a superstitious reverence for all manifestations of the printed word. Whatever the cause, the researcher should not believe everything he is told.

(iii) Third, many authorities are simply inadequate in themselves. They are lightweight, unreliable, obviously biased. To this category belong a variety of articles in the popular Press; unsupported and possibly garbled news reports; statements on the national policy culled from Party Political Manifestoes; puffs and pamphlets; certain works published under the great stresses of wartime pressures; works which are openly and blatantly confined to the grinding of a single axe. Such material, the biased and the trivial, may have a useful supporting role to play. No serious paper could be written around them as major sources.

SHAPE AND FLOW

(a) The aerodynamic shape, as it were, of the paper I have discussed in Chapter 4. A desirable shape is one in which the *natural form* of the topic has been discerned, and exploited. Failure to do this results in a paper that is as shapely as a sack or an amoeba. I find in practice two main varieties of this deformed shape. In the first variety, the basic structure is sound; but the treatment of a certain part of the paper may be over- or underdone. The bulkiness of a single part of the paper makes the whole work lop-sided; equally, a comparatively skimpy treatment leaves the reader frustrated and dissatisfied. Particularly is this true of topics with a historical basis. The researcher tends in his enthusiastic early phase to stockpile a mass of notes; the later periods may be less exhaustively treated. I have noted, for example, that papers dealing with the rise of the Trade Union movement tend to dwell at quite disproportionate length on the Tolpuddle Martyrs and the Taff Vale disputants. The writers are less inclined to devote their space to the problems confronting Mr. George Woodcock. The second variety of shapelessness concerns the inclusion of a side-issue. Sometimes the most eager researchers are guilty of this fault. They find themselves fascinated by an issue worth no more than a brief mention in the paper as a whole; devote considerable pains to covering the issue; and do not have the hardihood to excise this fascinating but irrelevant material. I repeat a warning I have given earlier; much, quite often most, research is wasted. One has to bear with this, and be ready to cut. To pursue the anatomical metaphor further, a paper should have a good bone-structure—and a good visual shape.

(b) On Flow, I draw the reader's attention to the remarks on page 39. Absence of flow indicates a stammering, disjointed paper. Apart from the guide-words ("however", "second-ly", and so on) which I have recommended, I should like to emphasize the value of headings. A paper which is divided into anonymous "Sections" and "Chapters" is much harder to follow than one with descriptive headings. The reader ought to be told exactly what is coming up. Moreover, he can make the mental adjustment far more easily if his eye is helped by spacings, underlinings, use of different coloured inks, and other aids. A little imagination in the exploitation of typographic resources makes a quite amazing difference to the reader's ready comprehension of a paper. Finally, the writer ought if possible to make his transitions easy, by referring in the first sentence of a new section to the position arrived at in the previous section.

PRESENTATION

Few, if any, products sell well unless they are seductively packaged. That is a blunt fact of modern life which it is useless to decry, and still more to ignore. A quite astonishing number of students, in my experience, view the matter differently. They are disposed to take the view that native worth, untrammelled by conventional presentation, is all. They are apt to regard conventional documentation, format, proof-reading, and even spelling, as in some way a betrayal of their integrity. With this view-point I have no desire to undertake a laboured disputation. There are perhaps two points to be made. First, courtesy to one's reader suggests that one make his task as easy as possible. The paper ought then to be a visual pleasure, properly typed and set forth in accordance with the conventions which the reader is entitled to expect. Second, the plainest self-interest demands that one's work be presented in the best possible light. Most of us, I imagine, know the feeling of drafting a passage in long-hand— which we think to be not very good—and after typing out the draft, revising our opinion upwards. Essentially the same work looks far better. It is impossible to evade the consequences of this simple psychological fact. I can see no point whatsoever in neglecting this simple logic: if the world judges by appearances, let the appearances be on one's side.

In practice this has two important implications. Care has to be devoted to the visual techniques of presentation: decent margins, ample spacings, well-judged headings, appropriate underlinings. Then, proof-reading should be absolute. This is the worst single chore an author has to tackle. There is no escape at all, but I strongly recommend that a colleague be induced, on a treaty of reciprocity, to duplicate one's proof-reading. The eye has a quite amazing capacity to miss the identical error a dozen times running. A fresh eye spots it immediately. It is worth the labour. The sense of irritation which a reader experiences, when he encounters an otherwise excellent work whose appearance is ruined by shoddy proof-reading, is not easily to be described. I have before me a major work, brought out by a reputable publisher, which contains three gross errors on the opening page. It is hard to see the labour of months let down badly for want of half-an-hour's concentrated proof-reading at the end.

There is one final point to make. The basic virtue of all research is accuracy. And for this virtue nobody's memory is sufficient; nobody's care in copying quotations is sufficient. Therefore, let all quotations be checked at the last. I end with the advice of Dr. Routh—all wisdom consists of truisms: "You will find it a very good practice always to verify your references, Sir!"